The Genius of Algorand

Also by Anthony Scaramucci

The Sweet Life with Bitcoin: How I Stopped Worrying about Cryptocurrency and You Should Too!

The Genius of Algorand

Technical Elegance and the DeFi Revolution

By Anthony Scaramucci

SALT Books
An Imprint of Post Hill Press
ISBN: 978-1-63758-871-0
ISBN (eBook): 978-1-63758-872-7

The Genius of Algorand:
Technical Elegance and the DeFi Revolution
© 2022 by Anthony Scaramucci
All Rights Reserved

Cover design by Tiffani Shea

Interior Design by Yoni Limor

Post Hill Press
New York • Nashville
posthillpress.com

Published in the United States of America
1 2 3 4 5 6 7 8 9 10

For AJ, Amelia, Anthony, Nicholas and James. The future has arrived early.

"Human beings are born solitary, but everywhere they are in chains—daisy chains—of interactivity. Social actions are makeshift forms, often courageous, sometimes ridiculous, always strange. And in a way, every social action is a negotiation."

- Andy Warhol, American artist

"There should be no such thing as boring mathematics."

- Edsger Dijkstra, Dutch systems scientist

"Collaboration always wins over competition—and is more fun, too."

- Silvio Micali, 2012 Turning Award Winner, Founder of Algorand Inc.

TABLE OF CONTENTS

CHAPTER 1

Anthony and the Algonauts

Here's the tightrope I've been walking when it comes to cryptocurrency and digital decentralized finance. I'm an institutionalist advisor with a roster of likeminded clients. Now, I must tell this wary group that there's a new way of doing business—it is coming like a wave and bringing unprecedented opportunities for those willing to get involved.

The blockchain revolution can't be explained without going back to the basics. "Blockchains" are information recorded and stored securely in groups or "blocks." Other users can add to these "blocks," forming a transparent but secure "chain" of information showing what was added, and when. As more blocks are added, the previous blocks provide a secure and immutable record or ledger of all previous transactions and other stored information. Many public blockchains store digital assets like stablecoins, NFTs and cryptocurrencies on their ledgers. These assets can be traded or transferred on the chain, creating a new economy unfettered by traditional obstacles and inefficiencies.

The blockchain is a game-changing technology, and exactly the kind of opportunity I need to be aware of on behalf of my clients. I founded Skybridge Capital in March 2005. The founding principle was to democratize the hedge fund space. A $50,000 investment in the hedge fund, SkyBridge, will give you what we believe is the best portfolio. We also bundle client money to gain access to elite funds with higher buy-ins. By 2022, we had 11,000 clients and $3.2 billion in assets.

Even though I started as a skeptic, I came to the realization that blockchain technology was going to change everything. At the start of 2021, my company launched the SkyBridge Bitcoin Fund. The pace of Bitcoin's acceptance has only increased since we launched the fund. For every price or regulatory setback—there have been some and will be more—there is evidence of expansion and adoption. (For more, see my previous book, "*The Sweet Life with Bitcoin.*")

Even as the SkyBridge Bitcoin Fund got off the ground in 2021, I recognized there is more to the blockchain story than seeing tokens as a better form of cash. They can also be programmed and used to convert asset ownership rights into a secure digital token on a blockchain. There is an entire world being created around applications creating new ways to use such tokenization. Pieces of anything can be traded electronically and monetized in an entirely new way, including regulated financial instruments like bonds and equities, as well as real estate, precious metals, and intellectual property. This is a full-on revolution; previously illiquid assets will be tokenized and eventually on exchanges.

One of my favorite examples is a platform called Lofty AI. A piece of real estate is tokenized, enabling investors to buy a piece for as little as $50. The person selling property ends up fetching a higher price and the people investing have access to a product that was previously out of reach. Matching these new buyers and sellers with no intermediaries creates new liquidity and with it, an opportunity for both sides to mutually benefit.

I think things are going to be even more liquid as blockchain introduces all sorts of efficiencies. (We will explore some compelling examples later in the book.) The opportunities are vast—authors, environmental groups, national governments, and banks have all vested interests in doing things differently. Really, when you think about it, only a small portion of the world is liquid.

There are more traditional segments of the economy that already have access to liquidity, but still see value in the blockchain because of its payment transparency and efficiency. Tokenization can reduce transaction times and even enable ceaseless trading triggered by predefined parameters. These instantaneous, completely peer-to-peer transactions are just one example of the ability of so-called "smart contracts" to transform a business model.

In 2021 it became my job to scour the crypto landscape for a digital token that will emerge from the pack as a dominant market winner. My main question, asked from the middle of the tightrope was, "What is going be the protocol that will best address the needs of large-scale institutions?"

The most natural place to turn would be Ethereum, which enjoys by far the largest market share of decentralized finance (DeFi) activity. Ethereum is an ingenious creation, but far from perfect. Vitalik Buterin, one of the co-founders of Ethereum, points out weaknesses by saying blockchains can only guarantee two of the following: decentralization, security, and scalability. Buterin calls this a "blockchain trilemma," an inherent limitation that comes with the blockchain.

Everything seemed to have a tradeoff: Pure decentralization, for example, costs speed. If a transaction requires multiple confirmations before reaching consensus, then inherently, it takes longer. In Ethereum's case, its network nodes verify every transaction before completing the block, making it inherently slow. Ethereum enables just 13 transactions per second (TPS) compared to its enormous daily demand of 1.355 million TPS, causing network congestion and high transaction gas fees.

Solving the trilemma is the holy grail of crypto. In the course of our analysis—after all these years, I'm still doing homework—I uncovered a protocol that has solved the equation. It's called Algorand. Algorand has the technological chops and intellectual pedigree to be a blockchain of the future.

When I say pedigree, I mean it. Algorand was co-founded by a living legend of cryptography, Silvio Micali. He's a Turing Award winner (that's like the Oscars of computer science or Nobel Prize, only harder to get) and the Ford Professor of Engineering at MIT, a pioneer of the discipline whose work is literally built into the foundation of all cryptocurrencies. Algorand was formed in 2017. Micali's approach solves the problems that emerged and fills a void in the marketplace of today and the future. We will hear him tell his story in less than a chapter.

I was also taken by the impact of the apps being designed. An increasing number of people were tapping Algorand for a wide range of uses, limited only by aspiration and imagination. Lofty AI is one of them. Algos have also been used to create things like new carbon credit marketplaces, tokenized artist catalogs and, in the case of the Marshall Islands, a new legal tender.

Reports and white papers only get you so far; the cornerstone of due diligence is human feedback, so I called my old boss, Bob Matza. He bought my first business, Oscar Capital, that I started with Andrew K. Boszhardt Jr. when we left Goldman Sachs. Bob is an advisor to Algorand and is someone with whom I could both explore the idea honestly and plan next steps.

Matza had a direct vantage on what I'd been hearing—Algorand offers a unique solution and is backed by a certified genius and an executive team with real vision. The best way to confirm this, I knew, was to speak with them directly. Zoom calls preceded a trip to Boston to meet Algorand Inc. Former COO and current interim CEO Sean Ford, and Former CEO Steve Kokinos. These were the first of what would become known as "Algonauts," a riff on the ancient Greek heroes who joined Jason to pursue the Golden Fleece.

Now you know why I was interested, but what would these executives want with me? Ask Ford, and he'll tell you they needed someone to help bring Algorand out of the shadows and drive mainstream institutional blockchain adoption. "We vetted potential candidates to take that step with and build a partnership," he says. "It certainly was the right time for us to kick things into gear and bridge the traditional blockchain world with the traditional financial institutional world into the decentralized digital environment of the blockchain, and Anthony is the perfect person to do that."

I had been a vocal advocate for cryptocurrency for a long time by the time I met Algorand's execs. When Skybridge launched the BTC fund, I debated everyone from Bill Maher to Janet Yellen in public forums. In private meetings, I explained and tutored crypto to clients, institutions, and anyone else who'd listen. SkyBridge even runs a Bitcoin node from our office. Those efforts didn't go unappreciated by Algorand, who above all needed an advocate to point out just how revolutionary the chain really is.

"Our focus has always been on building value in the company versus hyping the company," Ford concedes. "We overweighted building bulletproof technology. We have a relentless focus on building credibility, a credible product that works and a company that has long term value creation in its sights."

I left Boston feeling confident in the technology and the team. The big thing about serving clients well is being able to think like they do. Would very large institutions accept Algorand as a viable alternative to more popular blockchains like Ethereum? I believe the answer is "yes," of course there is room for both these and many other Layer-1 protocols. When chief technology officers at large corporations do a deep, extensive dive, like I did, they are often going to pick Silvio's blockchain.

Algorand is coming into the market a little late, and it appears small compared to other tokens. But I use an analogy to capture this moment. In an analogy to Web1 and the adoption of the internet, at this point, we were logging onto the Internet, using things like America Online to dial in. It worked, but not that well. If we have all these other ways to get on the internet, why do we need Google? Well, Google is faster, it has more broad search capability, and its algorithms incorporate machine learning that produces more relevant results. Guess what happened? Google eats everybody's lunch.

I think Algorand is Google. And I'm not alone. "Algorand is going to be the winner in building the backbone for what institutions need and financial services companies need," I told *CNBC* in September.

How I came to that conclusion, plus telling the full origin story of Algorand and describing its ability to reshape the future, is the purpose of this book. But first, let's answer a question for those who may be new to the topic.

Why Do We Need Crypto?

Creating new forms of currency and financial infrastructures seems a bold proposition. So, let's have a quick talk to destigmatize the concept, and consider how blockchain-backed assets are better forms of money.

There are pieces of paper (actually, our money is made from cloth but we all call it paper) with green ink in my pocket right now. And I can use those in the local shop to pay for a bottle of wine. If I have something that you trust in my hand serving as money, you're going to take it from me and convert it into other goods and services. There are various reasons to trust currency's worth—they can be backed by being tied to something rare but tangible, like gold. Or it can be floating, backed by the full faith and trust of the government that issues it, i.e., "fiat currency."

Only the trust in the discipline of the government backing it gives fiat currency value. Because of the COVID pandemic and a global financial crisis, we have a massive proliferation of fiat currency. When government prints more money, it usually ends in tears.

Politicians are relying on central bankers to smooth things over with low interest rates and by flushing the marketplace with liquidity. Asset reflation is exacerbating the economic stratification of American and global society. The wealthy are getting wealthier, because their assets are going up in nominal value, and because the poor and the middle class don't own any assets, they are getting left behind as their wages are being devalued due to inflation. As nations around the world devalue their currency for reasons of geopolitics and domestic pressure, users of that currency will suffer—and seek alternatives.

Every time humanity has embraced technology, whether from a horse and buggy to an electric car, or from telephone to video conference, we're moving ahead toward something better suited to the demands of the day. It makes sense that our money will also advance technologically.

The blockchain creates more stable forms of money. The concept of "scarcity" is key—something with a limited supply has more value. If an asteroid stuffed with gold landed on earth, the price of gold would plummet. If a government tinkers with its fiat currency or invites inflation through deficit spending and quantitative easing, the value of the currency it backs will change. In contrast, a well-run cryptocurrency has immutable, predetermined, mathematically certain scarcity.

A huge advantage of digital money comes when it's used to remove intermediaries and third parties—and eliminate all the expenses they accrue. Right now, we all use intermediaries to build trust into our everyday lives. Amazon serves as an intermediary whenever someone buys socks, shoes, books, or anything else through their portal.

But now, using the blockchain, I can transfer value without any intermediary. All the traditional steps are taken out of the process, leaving a truly peer-to-peer system. Banks are intermediaries. I tell you my bank is going to wire $5,000 to your bank account. You trust your bank. I trust my bank. Your bank trusts my bank. The money gets wired digitally, you now have that $5,000 in your account, and everybody believes that it happened. Now you can use that money to do what you want, but a lot of people have become involved in what is basically a one-on-one transfer.

In the real world, these are not an inconvenience, they are a major cost center. International payments and remittances, for example, take days and carry all types of fees and requirements. One of the big issues during a merger or real estate closing is making sure that money is transferred so titles can be exchanged. Even when using wire transfers, it can take hours or days to confirm money between banks. In comparison, electronic blockchain transactions take microseconds. In a cryptocurrency world, the confirmations are built into the transfer of the money.

That's why electronic confirmations happen very quickly—and cheaply—on the blockchain. This is true for massive oil shipments, but also applies when a newly retired couple rents a house in Italy for the summer. Imagine fees for credit cards, wire transfers, checks, and other expenses related to the movement of money becoming as extinct as cave bears.

Just as banks could be driven from the money-movement business, they may also be replaced as lenders. Banks, of course, collect money from many individuals as depositors and then lend out that capital. They charge interest or demand collateral, largely based on the risk they are assuming.

But, what if instead of a borrower applying to one bank, they borrow money from multiple people simultaneously through cryptocurrency and block-chain? Traditional means of assessing credit are outdated, and blockchain technology offers a 21st century solution of peer-to-peer loans priced based on on-chain data. Administrative costs and the difficulty of dividing fiat money has made such a system impractical. But blockchains remove those obstacles. It raises the possibility of a world without banks. This is the transformative nature of blockchain technology. I like to remind people that money is a tool. The Greek root of this word is "techno," making technology the study of tools. Technology can change currency as much as any other tool, replacing what we use when something better comes along. But these tools are not found; they are created. It's time to learn more about why Algorand is the most advanced and sustainable blockchain.

CHAPTER 2
Estimated Prophet

In 1979, Silvio Micali got off the airplane in San Francisco and was immediately confused. Fresh from Rome at age 24 and unable to speak English, he was desperate to find the shuttle that would bring him to his new life as a student at the University of California, Berkeley. "I had to ask seven people because nobody could understand me," Micali recalls. "I tell you the truth, I was terrified."

The young Sicilian studied mathematics in Rome but wanted to experience a less limiting perspective as he concentrated his higher education on computer science. "Every tradition is very rich, but also puts a box around what you can think about," he says. "I wanted to go someplace where I could start from scratch and help fill the need to be more creative."

The young man comes from a family of jurists. His father is a judge and siblings are lawyers. Micali went a different route, graduating from La Sapienza University in 1978. But something about his father's pursuit of truth, of verifying things with certainty in a sea of skeptical doubt, stuck with him. And Micali also admits that an obsession with keeping secrets might be ingrained in his Sicilian roots.

California wasn't easy for him. He was stuck in introductory classes with teenagers, isolated by a language barrier, and bereft of friends. Micali was tempted to head back to Italy, but was discovering new intellectual avenues. The last three lectures in a computational number theory class were focused on its applications to something called cryptography.

Cryptography, simply put, is the study of safe-guarding information to ensure that only the intended recipient understands it. With roots in code-breaking and wartime espionage, it's sort of a dark art. In modern times, as the information revolution continues to evolve, cryptography is fundamental to billions of people's daily lives. A few decades ago, however, it existed in a realm between disciplines. It's not really a subset of math or computer science, but employs principles from both. Luckily, Berkeley had an all-star roster of computer science faculty at the time and cryptography was something they encouraged students to ponder.

"I thought, wow, this is a very cool stuff," Micali says. "It was very appealing to me because nobody knew anything about it. And I usually I do better when there is a desert, no structures."

Micali also found support from the hidden culture that sustains Berkeley—students collab-orating with each other. A friend, his first one in the United States, asked why he didn't just focus on graduate-level courses instead of the regular checklist of undergraduate classes. "Just jump in and swim," Micali recalls the advice. "And that's what I did. When I enrolled again for the fall, I took a graduate course."

It was a game-changing move, for himself and the world. The moment came when the professor presented a challenging problem to the class aimed at a fundamental function: matching.

Every toddler, and a lot of other animals, can identify similar objects based on common properties. But matching is more complicated for mathematicians, who seem to enjoy building elaborate graphs to determine the best way to map unique relationships between many objects.

One basic way to envision matching as a mathematical problem is by pretending you're a boss with a staff, and each worker needs to be paired with a specific job. A staff of five doesn't pose much of a cognitive problem, but these problems get complex when the number of people and jobs (called nodes) increases. Matching five-million jobs with five-million people takes a powerful algorithm, and one that can work fast to be of any use. These academic tributaries in the late 1970's would soon have major implications. The era of vast social networks and a globally-connected Internet was on the horizon.

Micali's professor tasked his students with a basic but fundamental challenge: Find the fastest way to solve a general matching problem. He and a grad student named Umesh Virkumar Vazirani became obsessed. "I stopped listening to all courses and I focused on solving that problem," Micali says.

Their solution became the most efficient algorithm known for general matching. The trick of the "MV Algorithm" (as it's known) is that it operates in phases, searching collections of nodes for one that satisfies a given property. If you picture the nodes hanging like fruit on a tree, the algorithms have precise ways of scouring specific branches for matches, and for not searching the same limb more than once. That's pretty dumbed down but going deeper can make your brain ache and eyes bleed.

Micali and Vazirani published their algorithm in 1980. It was a huge moment for the young Italian mathematician, one that helped establish him as a leading light in the rapidly changing field of cryptography. As a student, however, his ground-breaking work was subpar. Because his initial results lacked proper proof, Micali received a B+ in the graduate course from the professor who gave him the matching challenge.

More important than his GPA, Micali had found his calling as a trailblazer in the field of modern cryptography. "I decided to dedicate myself to that stuff," he says. "Why? Because I was fearless and I found another fearless traveling companion in my long-life friend, Shari Goldwasser."

Born in New York City, Goldwasser obtained her Bachelor of Science degree in 1979 in mathematics and science from Carnegie Mellon University. By 1981, she already had a Master of Science degree from Berkeley.

When they met, Goldwasser was a fellow grad-uate student doing research under the supervision of Manuel Blum, a Venezuelan American computer scientist who received the Turing Award in 1995. He was one of the word's leaders who built the foun-dations of computational complexity theory. Blum would devise ways to study problems and quantify the number of resources an algorithm would need to solve them, such as time, storage, or the number of gates in a computer. This all speaks to one of the key tenants of computational complexity—to determine the practical limits on what computers can do.

Goldwasser shared Micali's fascination with what algorithms could accomplish. However, things were changing when it came to using them to encrypt systems. In the late 1970's, ciphers were starting to turn away from the traditional symmetric key algorithms, i.e., using a key that unlocks the information that must be shared between the sender and recipient. That may be alright between two people but try scaling that up to a multitude of users and the security and efficiency of the symmetric key algorithm plummets.

So how do you prove an interaction between two parties has occurred without compromising their privacy? In cryptography, the idea of "proof" is a never-ending quest, the product of the algorithmic machinery Goldwasser and Micali had to invent.

"We said, we are going to solve this, and turns out actually we did solve it, but it took 10 years," Micali says. "Somehow, we invented this notion of how to encrypt without leaking any partial information. We were lucky in being myopic, and not seeing how difficult it was."

What they invented was the technique of probabilistic encryption, which generates the randomness in an encryption algorithm called a "zero-knowledge proof." To explain this may take some creative writing, and a secretive gnome.

The Secret Door

A cryptography textbook will define a zero-knowledge proof as "a method by which one party (the prover) can prove to another party (the verifier) that a given statement is true while the prover avoids conveying any additional information apart from the fact that the statement is indeed true." I find it easier to understand by borrowing from Jean-Jacques Quisquater, who in 1989 wrote a paper called "How to Explain Zero-Knowledge Protocols to Your Children."

In my version, a lady gnome possesses a secret word used to open a magic door in a cave. The cave is circular, with the entrance on one side and a magic door blocking the opposite side. A guy named Alex wants to know whether the gnome knows the secret word that opens the door, but the wily critter does not want to reveal the secret word to Alex or reveal the fact she knows it to the non-magic world in general.

Here's what they decide to do. They label the left and right paths from the entrance A and B. First, Alex waits outside the cave as the gnome goes in. The gnome takes either path A or B; Alex is not allowed to see which path she takes. Then, Alex enters the cave and shouts the name of the path he wants her to use to return, either A or B, chosen at random. Providing she really does know the magic word, this is easy, and she'll return along the requested path.

However, suppose the gnome is a liar and doesn't know the word. Then, she would only be able to return through the named path if Alex were to give the name of the same path by which she had entered. Since Alex would choose A or B at random, she would have a 50 percent chance of guessing correctly. The gnome's chance of successfully anticipating all of Alex's requests will continually plummet the more times the process repeats. If the gnome repeatedly appears at the exits Alex names, anyone could conclude that she does know the secret word.

Enough with this mythic creature. Micali and Goldwasser used this kind of zero-knowledge randomization to create an encryption tool called a "Verifiable Random Function." VRF outputs can be proven to be correct without any information being divulged, and it's an algorithm that can be calculated quickly. Modern applications include digital cash, password-authenticated key agreements, and time-stamping services. VRF makes digital signatures possible since any signature can be bound to the original message with mathematical certitude.

In other words, VRF is at the heart of our modern digital world. "Silvio has either helped invent or participated in the creation of public key cryptography, which is what secures the internet and banking system," says Steve Kokinos, "and he's invented a lot of the things used in every blockchain, not just Algorand." The verification without trust will always come from the randomized math.

But in 1982, this was just part of Micali's PhD in computer science from Berkeley. After receiving it, he began to cast his eyes east. Micali and Goldwasser both joined MIT in 1983. It was a different environment—more competitive, contentious, and ambitious. Micali enjoyed the institution's ethos of tackling impossible problems. He and Goldwasser continued their longstanding collaboration and built the early, transformative cryptography curriculum. (The pair remain close; she serves as an advisor to Algorand.)

When it came to verifiable random functions, Micali says he knew they'd be useful somehow, but he didn't dwell on developing commercial applications: "The deep-down conviction that I was working on was something that the world needs was always there," he says. "I knew from the very beginning that this is going to be the bread and butter and the foundation of everything that we are going to do going forward in security and finance. I knew for sure. But on the other hand, I was theoretical. If someone said, 'You want to prove one more theorem or go and consult for Citi Corp,' it's an easy decision. I'd prove the theorem. But at some point, something changed."

What changed was the blockchain revolution.

Working the Problem

In 2012, Micali was enjoying life as a celebrated mathematician and MIT professor. His wall was already decorated with accolades, including the Gödel Prize in 1993 and RSA Award for Excellence in Mathematics in 2004. His National Academy of Sciences membership came in 2007. Over the years, Micali created the modern study of cryptography as it applies to the digital age. His students included a litany of future bright lights in the field. "The secret to teaching, and don't tell anyone, is that you learn more from your students than they learn from you," Micali says.

In 2012, Micali and Goldwasser received the Turing award for their work in cryptography. But Micali was keeping his eye on how their mathematical breakthroughs were manifesting in the real world, particularly with the rise of cryptocurrencies. The inventor was hearing details about what people were doing with his creations while he toiled inside the lab and university.

As time went on, some limitations were on display. Bitcoin is secure, but its processes are also relatively slow. Ethereum is faster but lacks the same level of decentralization when it comes to who validates transactions. Micali finds blockchain splitting ("forking"), by necessity or rebellion, an inelegant practice. (We will discuss this in more depth later.) Other coins were birthed just to be traded, including pump-and-dump, flash-in-the-pan players. People were talking about the trilemma of decentralization, security, and scalability as if it were an impossible quest.

But Micali believed the right blockchain protocol could deliver all three. It was just the kind of thorny, impossible question that caught his attention. "I thought it was marvelous," Micali says, "so, at that point I locked myself in a in a room for a month to work the problem."

The white paper that resulted from that lonely, intensive time was titled "Algorand" and authored by Micali and Jing Chen[1], dated July 4, 2016. Each blockchain has its own currency or token; Algorand's is called Algo. The abstract lays out the ground-breaking aspects in flat, academic prose:

> "A public ledger is a tamperproof sequence of data that can be read and augmented by everyone. Public ledgers have innumerable and compelling uses. They can secure, in plain sight, all kinds of transactions— such as titles, sales, and payments— in the exact order in which they occur. Public ledgers not only curb corruption but also enable very sophisticated

---

1   Chen attended MIT from 2007 to 2012 and received a double PhD in Computer Science and Philosophy. She is currently Chief Scientist at Algorand, LLC.

applications such as cryptocurrencies and smart contracts. They stand to revolutionize the way a democratic society operates. As currently implemented, however, they scale poorly and cannot achieve their potential. Algorand is a truly democratic and efficient way to implement a public ledger. Unlike prior implementations based on proof of work, it requires a negligible amount of computation and generates a blockchain that will not fork with overwhelmingly high probability."

The paper notes that Algorand is based on "a novel and super-fast message-passing Byzantine agreement." The name is derived from a historical problem involving issuing orders to a collection of loyal and disloyal generals from Byzantium. The core problem is protecting a system of communication even when bad actors are present. In distributed computing, it means all processors can agree on a common value, even if some components are corrupt.

In traditional Byzantine agreements, users agree on one of their starting values, a way to verify the information is going to the authorized recipient. In a Byzantine agreement with "leader election," a small but always changing committee of users agrees on a value proposed by a leader.

This is highly relevant given the way Algorand works. Rather than giving the power to validate new blocks to the people with the most coins, Algorand holds lightning-fast cryptographic lotteries to generate randomness.

Owners of at least 1,000 tokens (out of the 10 billion in circulation) randomly validate the next block. Anyone in the world who owns Algos can participate in consensus. Every block produces a new random selection seed, and a user secretly checks whether they were selected to participate in the consensus protocol by evaluating a VRF with their secret participation key and the selection seed.

This also produces a proof, which the user can send to anyone to show that they have been selected to participate, like proving the gnome knew the magic word by showing how many times the creature accessed the door in that cave. Accounts are selected to propose blocks for a given round, with no single target presented to hackers and no way malicious users can gain advantages by registering multiple accounts.

On Algorand, blocks are produced every 4.5 seconds and can hold up to 5,000 transactions, which results in a throughput of about 1,000 transactions per second. Upgrades will soon boost these numbers to 10,000 transactions in under 2.5 seconds. That speed comes with an additional benefit in that it requires little computing power and therefore has negligible negative environmental impact. (We'll explore that aspect in depth later since it's so important.)

"Scaling is not enough," Micali says, "If it scales and is not cheap, not everybody can take advantage. A fraction of a cent is about the right price because everybody can absorb it. Typically, the centralized economy is very expensive, and I cannot see a mediator to help two farmers in two places in the world interacting from afar. But now, you can really have a common marketplace."

Micali put his 75-page white paper on the web as soon as it was finished; this marked the first time he'd taken that step instead of publishing a work or presenting it at a conference. Micali says, "Strangely enough, the first person who reads it and knocks on my door was an MIT colleague.... He says, 'It is too good to be true. I think we should test it.' No surprise, his test was very rigorous."

The protocol that Micali proposed was solid. He'd created a new tool for the modern age—one that solves some of the main drawbacks of cryptocurrency and improves its benefits. "At this point... do I want to wait here another 25 years to see this emerge? I don't think so," Micali says. "We decided to start a company."

Algonauts Assemble

In 2016, Steve Kokinos was mulling the evolution of the crypto world. The successful Boston-based entrepreneur's friends included early Bitcoin miners, and they were after him to get involved in blockchain.

"I found that both the tech and philosophical underpinnings were really fascinating," he recalls. "They were the most like anything I had seen in the early days of the Internet."

Kokinos is a serial entrepreneur, who holds the co-founder and executive chairman positions at Fuze, a transformative cloud communications provider. Fuze now has more than 1500 customers around the world. He also co-founded BladeLogic, a leader in the data center automation market with a Fortune 500 client list. BladeLogic held a successful IPO, and BMC Software acquired it for around $800 million.

It's fair to say that Kokinos has a keen eye for future opportunities. He does his homework too. As he surveyed the crypto space in 2016, he reached out to a brain trust of friends at the venture capital firm Union Square Ventures. They told him about something called Algorand.

"They said, 'If you're going do something in the space, Silvio is really the 'OG of crypto,'" Kokinos recalls, 'And it seems like he's going to do something.'"

One afternoon soon after, he walked over to Micali's office at MIT for a sit down. It was hard not to be impressed. "In Italy, he's like a national hero," Kokinos says. "He's like the most famous living Italian scientist. There's no cryptographer or distributed computer scientist in the world that doesn't owe a debt to that guy's inventions."

It wasn't his accolades but his new idea that really struck Kokinos. "I was really impressed by the way Silvio rethought some of the fundamental problems in computer science and how you might apply those to a new blockchain network," he says. "Algorand in a lot of ways really represented kind of a completely new approach."

In 2017, Micali founded Algorand, with Kokinos as the CEO. "We feel it's necessary to bring an increasing percentage of the world's financial trans- actions onto public blockchains," he says of the company's overall mission.

Just how to go about that mission became the subject of much debate at Micali's home, which became the home to Algorand's founders and servers. "The developers were in the dining room, we never had guests for dinner for a long time," he recalls. "The living room was the all-hands area where we had all the discussions."

Debates flared in the living room. The Master of Mathematical consensus had to reach a more real-world form of consensus with his team members. Micali found the intense collaboration stimulating and productive. It was a new territory for the mathematician, who was no longer working in solitude. "I'd never been part of a company, and I didn't know how much joint effort is required and how much you can think of collectively," he says.

One major focus of discussions was how to make sure the applications on the network were as decentralized, scalable, and secure as Algorand itself. "You need all that at a fundamental level, but you also need that in how you build applications," says Kokinos.

We will spend a lot of this book exploring the many real-world uses of Algorand apps, so it'll be helpful to be familiar with the tools they're built on. The term "smart contract" is central to the way Algorand builds an ecosystem of users. These are so-called "trustless programs" where users can be confident that the program was executed without error and results untampered. Smart contracts can self-execute based on predefined conditions in their code, in some cases eliminating the need for central authorities and intermediaries like lawyers. The contracts have since been used to enable multiple, simultaneous financial transactions, build a market-place for small purchases of gold, and collect crowd investments in startups.

Smart contracts in Algorand are written in a language called Transaction Execution Approval Language (TEAL). Algorand's Virtual Machine suite interprets TEAL programs, a set of operation codes used in smart contracts and smart signatures. Using these, organizations can now quickly and inexpensively develop their own dApps. There's an overlay that bridges TEAL with the programming language Python.

Algorand got off to a slow start. The initial coin offering misfired since there wasn't a strong enough community around it. However, this is the purest, best technology for a Layer-1 protocol. I am not saying that the other Layer-1 protocols won't exist, but this one certainly will. The current (July 2022) market capitalization of Algo is nearly $2 billion, making it the 31st largest cryptocurrency in circulation.

Algo is not the biggest cryptocurrency out there, but the numbers are impressive and growing. They've created more than 20 million wallets, most of which were created in 2021, and a couple million transactions per day are executed on the network. Roughly 11,000 developers are building dApps on the platform.

The aspiration is to grow the network to hundreds of millions of wallets over the next two years, and the real-world uses are one key. "I think it's going to take some applications hitting mainstream a little bit more heavily to really gain that next level of user adoption," Kokinos says.

One thing you hear a lot among the Algorand community is that they are often regarded as the adults in the room compared to some other crypto offerings. They aren't flashy, they don't engage in superficial hype, and they tend to be forthright when it comes to real-world headwinds.

When you talk to Sean Ford about this, he uses his hands to trace two lines travelling in opposite directions until they converge into an X. "I go back to the speculation and substance," he says. "Speculation is driving the value less and technology will drive value more. At the end of the day, there has to be a correlation between long term value and the quality and trustworthiness of the tech."

Ford continues, "As more blockchain and cryptocurrencies become more mainstream and as more traditional investment and traditional capital enters the market, it's going to create stability. More importantly, it's going to create a level of rigor, for which most blockchain crypto projects are totally unprepared." He adds, "I can't wait. Bring on the institutional capital, bring on big investors, bring on the people that are going to really pressure test. Ultimately, that's going to make people care about the technology more than the hype."

Ford takes it a step further. "Algorand's goal is to become invisible. The more the technology, the application, or the device gets in the way of users doing what they want is the degree to which that it has failed."

Built to Last

The cryptocurrency world has a tribal element to it. Backers of a coin will live and die for it, just as those who believe in crypto feel locked in a struggle against the status quo. But the truth is that the crypto market, to be truly transformative, will depend on several dominant coins.

I think there will be winners--plural. It won't just be Algorand. I recognize that there will likely be room for other "Layer-1's,"[2] but I think Algorand

---

2   There are two primary ways to achieve blockchain scalability: Layer-1 and Layer-2 solutions. Layer-1 adds utility to a native blockchain to optimize its performance. Layer-2 solutions are third-party protocols that integrate with an underlying Layer-1 blockchain to increase transactional throughput.

will be the leading one. Could there be success for Solana and continued success for Ethereum? Yes, but I do think that Algorand will leapfrog the others.

It's an important point to make as we discuss the advantages of Algorand, which not only coexists with other coins but has been involved in building ways users can easily cross-utilize various cryptocurrencies. Still, the elegant solution devised by Silvio Micali has some real-world ramifications that make it such an attractive prospect, and it's easiest to see those advantages in comparison to other coins. No offense meant!

The key to any crypto architecture is the way it replaces a central authority to validate transactions. Bitcoin uses an approach known as "proof of work." All the aspiring validators on these networks are competing to be the first to solve a complex problem. If they are the first to prove their work, they can add the latest batch of transactions to the blockchain and thereby earn currency. The "miners" who emerge victorious are the ones with the most powerful computers.

However, some platforms use a method called proof of stake. Cryptocurrency holders "vote" to approve legitimate transactions. As a reward for voting on legitimate transactions, the voters are slowly paid in newly created cryptocurrency. Algorand is not the only player who has adopted the proof of stake approach; Ethereum, Solana, Avalanche, and Cardano have also adopted some form of "proof of stake" validation.

Proof of stake is faster than proof of work since transactions and blocks can be approved without any complex equations being solved. But such speed has usually come at the expense of decentralization and security, as dictated by the pesky trilemma. Algorand is built differently. The lighting fast elections of validators is "pure proof of stake" and completely decentralized, and thereby as secure as it is fast. The scalability and security are unmatched by other coins, and it's been designed to be a truly democratic way to implement a public ledger.

"Forking" is when a blockchain diverges into two separate paths. Sometimes, forking is intentional, like when a significant part of the community wants to change the fundamentals of the protocol. Other times, forking occurs when two miners find a block at nearly the same time. Eventually, one of the paths will be abandoned, and all transactions on the orphaned chain will be invalid.

The upshot: In a proof-of-work blockchain, transactions can't be considered final until a certain amount of time goes by. Since Algorand is pure proof-of-stake and uses a voting mechanism to validate blocks, forking is impossible. Transactions are final as soon as they are confirmed.

"We definitely think that the technology is going to matter a lot, whether it's national projects or larger institutional projects," says Ford. "Those people are doing deep dives into the technology and trying to understand what's there. That's why I think we're winning a lot of deals; people who really try to understand what's going on realize that our network works in a different way."

There is another large benefit to Algorand's pure proof of stake system that answers a common concern about cryptocurrency in general: its impact on the environment. Algorand was built to be a green coin. The energy required to run a node in its network is negligible and can be done on a device as simple as a Raspberry Pi. Compared to proof of work blockchains, digital asset creation and transactions on Algorand result in about two million times fewer CO_2 emissions.

Micali's impulse to tackle intractable problems still drives the company, and this time the question was how to measure the environmental impact of a global, decentralized, and widely used blockchain. In 2021, Algorand partnered with ClimateTrade, a Spanish fintech whose main objective is to help companies use the blockchain to achieve their sustainability goals by offsetting CO_2 emissions and financing climate change projects.

To achieve a carbon-negative network, Algorand and ClimateTrade will implement a sustainability oracle which will notarize Algorand's carbon footprint for each of a set number of blocks. With smart contracts, Algorand will then lock the equivalent amount of carbon credits as an Algo asset into a green treasury. This will enable the protocol to keep running as carbon negative.

"Algorand is experiencing accelerated adoption and network expansion," says Micali. "As this period of hyper growth continues, we find it crucial to operate at a carbon-negative level. Indeed, sustainable growth is way better than growth."

The Coming Upgrade Wars

In June 2021, I met up with Jeff Schumacher, the founder of the New Asset Exchange (NAX) in Los Angeles. Schumacher had just gotten back from the Bitcoin Miami conference. Over the course of the conversation, I asked if he heard of Algorand. "Interestingly enough," he says, "I just got back from their offices in Boston."

As an investment advisor and manager of a "fund of funds," I'm used to doing my research, forming a plan, and following through with confidence. But I'd be lying if I said I wasn't happy to hear that Jeff, who is a successful entrepreneur, had simultaneously reached the same conclusion that I did based on our discreet due diligence. Every choice for Algorand is a testament to its technology. "From a capitalistic standpoint," says NAX's director Ted Kraus of Level 1 protocols, "it's going to be hard to beat."

That's not to say that Algorand can't play nice with other Layer-1's. Just the opposite—there are many blockchain enabled apps that can run their transactions on the fast, secure Algorand. "This is why bridges are so important," he says.

The landscape will be very competitive, however. Ethereum and others are planning upgrades to reduce price and increase speed. These are retro-fits built on top of existing systems, while Algorand is built for these kinds of speed and links between nodes from the ground up. With Algorand, the primitives are all ready for Web 3.0, so you don't have to have these Layer Twos built on top.

The improvements for Algorand are going to put them heads and tails (Coin humor, get it?) above other tokens. One focus is on blockchain interoperability, creating new ways to forge the future of chain-to-chain communication. Developers will get lots of attention, with contract-to-contract calls, enhanced storage, and sophisticated smart contracts. The network's throughput is also expected to increase with new optimizations and reduced transaction settlement times.

So let the upgrade wars begin. Algorand is in prime position to win them. Over the next few years, there will be high profile upgrades to other protocols; some will work, others won't. Even if ETH ticks up in terms of speed and cost, it's still not going to be really where Algorand is now. The tech is cheaper, better, faster. It just goes back to the basics. When Algorand unleashes its upgrades, I think it's going to blow everybody else out of the water.

CHAPTER 3
Adopters of Algo

Outreach at Algorand means casting a wide net. "What's interesting about this space is that there's such a variety of audiences you have to speak to," says Keli Callaghan, formerly with Algorand but now with Arrington Capital. "It's a college student who wants to build blockchain initiatives and apply to an accelerator or incubator, countries that have billion-dollar economies, and everybody in between." Considering that, here's a quick survey of some of Algorand's users, broken into some helpful (if overlapping) categories.

Governments

In June 2021, Bermuda took the step to transform its healthcare system by embracing blockchains. They announced they've tapped the global healthcare technology firm, MAPay, to introduce a stablecoin to improve the efficiency of the healthcare system on. The healthcare payment system built on Algorand's blockchain network has the capacity to move $800 million in traditional healthcare payments to the blockchain.

The improvements will be felt by the whole nation. Traditional healthcare payment systems are cumbersome, but MAPay can seamlessly link insurance companies, government health providers, and banks without intermediaries. "Our relationship with Algorand is a global-game changer in healthcare commerce and data exchange," said MAPay CEO Michael Dershem. "Not only is our tech in alignment, but just as important, if not more so, our collective management vision and passion is spot-on."

There is increasing interest by governments in adopting blockchain technology, and Algorand offers a lot of what they're looking for. In March 2020, the Republic of the Marshall Islands became the first country to adopt a national digital currency. The SOV, backed by Algorand, would circulate alongside the U.S. dollar, upon which the nation had been previously dependent. Keep in mind that Western Union charges five dollars to send even small amounts of money from the Marshall Islands to the United States. Western Union fees can amount to 7 to 10 percent of a transaction.

El Salvador is also using Algorand for record-keeping, even as they try to use both Bitcoin and the U.S. dollar as legal tender. In August 2021, Koibanx, a leading Latin American financial infrastructure company, announced a cooperation agreement with the government there to develop its blockchain infrastructure.

The COVID-19 crisis made plain—and accelerated—some unsettling trends regarding the stability of government backed (or "fiat") currency. Governments proved unable to help themselves and will continue to print money to competitively debase their currencies and monetize the debt that they've taken on. If you can do this in a measured way, you can work your way out of a lot of debt. Unfortunately, it usually breaks out of control.

Money printing is a silent tax due to the inflation it creates. "The very idea of [money printing] tends to explode the heads of those who say dollars should come from work, savings, and investment instead of thin air," reads one *USA Today* article describing the situation in 2020. "In the age of a nearly $25 trillion national debt, such 'sound money' concepts seem outdated—relics of a bygone era in which the value of a dollar once was based on a fixed amount of gold."

By the end of 2020, the Fed purchased $3.5 trillion in government securities with newly created dollars. This came at a time when federal debt surpassed GDP and is projected to approach 109 percent of GDP by the end of 2021. General government debt will reach 127 percent of GDP in 2021 and surpass 130 percent by 2023. The only way a government can find a way out of this kind of debt is to devalue their currency through inflation.

Unsurprisingly, the early government adopters of the blockchain have been those who suffered from runaway inflation and economic uncertainty. Cryptocurrencies have become a lifeline for citizens at all economic levels as a way for them to reassert control over their financial lives. "Whether it's Latin America, where we're seeing a lot of adoption, or Southeast Asia or Africa, people's first exposure to modern financial tools will be through DeFi and crypto," says Ford. "They'll probably never have a bank account."

There is a natural hesitancy for governments to jump into crypto markets, but many are dipping their toes in the water. Panama, like Bermuda, is putting hundreds of millions of dollars' worth of healthcare payments on Algorand between insurance companies, hospitals, and the government.

In September 2021, the Colombian government needed an official immunization certificate for COVID. It chose Vitalpass, a digital vaccination passport created by Auna Ideas Foundation and Koibanx, developed leveraging Algorand's blockchain. Vitalpass records and certifies the vaccination status of citizens and connects with other vaccination passports globally. Dr. Andrés Vásquez, Auna's director of biomedical innovation and health-tech says, "The use of blockchain technology makes this digital passport one of the safest and most reliable tools to guarantee the transparent process of vaccination in Colombia, because the information cannot be changed, erased, or manipulated, thus ensuring the validity of the certificate against cases of forgery, double vaccination, or others."

These are not entire national economies, but these segments are vital trial runs for wider adoption. Algorand, built to be fast, secure, and stable at any size, brings welcome gravitas to a bold move. "Governments tend to find us very comfortable to work with because we have real people that can speak their language," Ford says, "and it's the technology. It isn't a case of, 'Just trust us.' We're in a situation where they find comfort in our focus on a long-term play."

While we're on the topic of enticing gun-shy entities into the world of crypto, let's take a look at Algorand's appeal in the conventional realm.

Traditional Finance

Institutions have built long-standing relationships with the intermediaries that enable transactions. Their dependency comes at a price, however, and that opens the door for the blockchain. "The potential efficiency gains and democratization of finance associated with DeFi are attractive to traditional financial institutions," Samantha Pelosi, a senior vice president at BAFT (the largest trade association for transaction banking) recently said in an article posted by the World Economic Forum. "However, DeFi negates the need for relationships with trusted intermediaries, which makes the model disruptive and somewhat alien to these banks."[3]

Bringing crypto back to Earth is part of my job, and nothing is as grounding as the story of Algorand. Micali's pedigree, his long-term strategy, and his understated marketing approach all ease any jitters institutions feel about the sometimes-chaotic world of crypto. "Financial institutions went from a person behind the counter to then ATM to then virtual banking," Ford says. "They did some of it because it was innovative and their customers found it interesting, but underneath it all's revenue growth."

Customers often win when these innovations take root. For example, take remittances: money transferred between national borders. During 2020

---

3   Rebecca Liao, "How decentralized finance will transform business financial services – especially for SMEs," *World Economic Forum*, July 2021, via: https://www.weforum.org/agenda/2021/07/decentralized-finance-transaction-banking-smes/

alone, people in Spain sent more than $18 billion dollars in remittances, most of it landing with their extended families Latin America. Moving the money requires running an inconvenient gauntlet of handlers who charge fees.

Now the fintech company Bnext is using Algorand's infrastructure to make these transactions cheaper and faster. Bnext executive Cristian Huertas calls it "the first step to expand inclusive financial product offerings that are convenient and recurrent to immigrants that have been exploited by traditional remittance companies."

Bnext, with more than 700,000 users, is the most prominent marketplace of financial services in Spain and Latin America. That's a large company adopting crypto to reshape the way business is done across borders. "That's an example of where traditional finance and decentralized finance sort of intersect," Ford says. "And that line is getting blurrier and blurrier as we go on, which is great."

The potential for institutions to make a difference in Algorand's development is hard to exaggerate. "If just one major bank with a huge real estate holding decides that they're going to issue a security token with collateral, backed with those real estate holdings, you're talking trillions of dollars," Ford says. "I think the biggest inflection points will be when you see the flagship, institutional products start to adopt blockchain technology."

The future looks very bright. In December 2021, Securitize Markets announced the launch of two tokenized funds on the S&P Dow Jones Indices. The new indices, the Cryptocurrency Large Cap Ex-MegaCap Index and the Kensho New Economies Composite Index, are tokenized using the Algorand protocol. They are the first tokenized funds to be listed by a major index provider.

This watershed moment is striking proof of the demand from leading financial institutions to adopt blockchain technology. "S&P DJI's innovation and leadership in tokenizing its indices is a major sign that institutions understand the many advantages of tokenization--from efficiency to easier investor access," said Scott Harrigan, CEO of Securitize Markets. "I anticipate this will be the start of a wave of tokenized funds."

Algorand is perfectly positioned to ride this wave.

Small and Startup DeFi

If you stop to think about it, the only ones with ready access to top tier banking services are big companies—their top customers. Centralized systems built to communicate with one another make possible all kinds of corporate transactions, such as supply chain finance and credit arbitrage. They see the blockchain largely as a new way to be more efficient (such as cutting costs and delays) and unlock frozen liquidity thereby making more money from assets that are dormant.

Lost in the mix are small and medium enterprises, or SMEs. They never had the access to traditional credit and transactional services that the big boys enjoy every day. To survive the modern age, they need more options. I have stats to back this up: a 2020 report by the World Trade Organization puts the shortfall in financing for SMEs at *$5 trillion*.

This figure represents a massive opportunity, one that the blockchain can fully meet since DeFi facilitates the fast, cheap exchange of trustable data. With that ability, developers are limited only by their imagination of what they can do to assist SMEs.

The appeal is clear: a small business owner doesn't have the resources to complete anti-money laundering and other "know your customer" checks on every source of capital. Nor would they have the network to present ready evidence of their payables and debts for each source, all of which would have to agree on one transaction ledger, or the business would have to have several, making a mess of its bookkeeping.

Yieldly was the world's first borderless and interconnected DeFi platform to be designed and developed on Algorand. Its professed mission is to empower a billion crypto users to exchange digital value without friction or security risk. Yieldly is backed by top venture capital firms, including Borderless Capital, LongHash Ventures, and CMS Holdings.

There are now a multitude of startup DeFi applications and gaining traction on Algorand. "I think some people come out of these accelerators and incubators with a different take on what finance means," says Ford. "It's not necessarily the same mixed portfolio, stocks, bonds, and that stuff. They say, 'Bank accounts don't earn you interest; what else can we do?'"

The universe of dApps that followed is fun to browse. There's Meld Gold, delivering real time access to a new population of auric investors and sparing them some of the volatility in that market. Republic is a private investing platform that lets anyone invest in early-stage companies. Chainanalysis provides blockchain data and analysis to government agencies, exchanges, and financial institutions across 40 countries. Algofi, whose founders we will meet later, is a fast, low-cost crypto lending market that opens decentralized lending in real estate.

"We've gotten to a point where, there's two or three businesses a week launching, and we have no idea we're they came from," Ford says. "People just come to build, which is a great place to be."

Creators and Artists

The Italian Society for Authors and Editors was founded in 1882 after the creative class organized to avoid exploitation, something much worse in modern times as conglomerates control more content. The result is a complex copyright jungle where royalties for artists are poached by publishers, lawyers, auditors, and other intermediaries. Now, the ISAE's 100,000 artists have their copyrights digitally represented and can trade or sell those rights at publicly listed market prices on Algorand's blockchain.

Big changes like this coming to the creator economy. Whether its physical pieces, digital art, or music, new markets with the absence of middlemen are empowering artists. "You can create a piece of art, put it into a smart contract, sell it yourself," Callagan says. "There is no gallery to approve a showing and take a percentage...and then, because it's in the smart contract, every time it sells on a secondary market, you get a commission. And that automatically happens, the tech does all of that."

Blockchain technology is democratizing both the digital and physical arts. There's a new array of community art rising, where different contributions of digital art are combined and sold. Some of the best artists in the world are participating in high-end NFT auctions. Artists are finding more ways to market their work. Peer-to-peer interactions also changes the relationship between fans and artists, previously something that has only been monetized through ticket and product sales. Now there's a new way to interact with, and profit from, a follower base.

"One of the things that blockchain and crypto has revealed is that there is like real financial value to the way a community rallies around different projects," says Steve Kokinos. "Music is sort of an interesting case because musicians by definition have always had these communities, which is their fan base...That has been either misunderstood or not properly accounted in most sort of traditional economic relationships."

Take, for example, Opulous, built on the Algorand chain. In November 2021, Lil Pump offered fans the chance to invest in his single, "Mona Lisa," featuring Soulja Boy and produced by Jimmy Duval. After just two hours of being publicly available, the track reached its maximum funding goal, selling out at $500,000 to 927 investors.

In December 2021, the music synchronization licensing marketplace, Dequency, executed the first-ever sync license on a public blockchain. Built with Web 3.0 technology, Dequency's mission is to connect visual creators directly with recording artists and other music rightsholders to create a simple and transparent licensing experience. It's a great example of creators gaining income-generating opportunities with minimal fees. The inaugural artist was Goldfish. "Being part of the very first sync is a real honor, and we cannot wait for the future as the music industry," he said.

The world of fine arts is also getting involved. The Los Angeles County Museum of Art, the largest art museum in the western United States, has teamed up with a selection of artists and tech companies to create a virtual exhibition that will be minted as an edition of NFT's on the Algorand block-chain. Participating artists include Lukas Avendaño, Jacqueline Kiyomi Gork, Rhett LaRue, Lawerence Lek, Jen Liu Ronald Rael, and Virginia San Fratello.

Gaming

Keli Callaghan isn't a fan of the type of promotional flair that has become popular in crypto circles. "We don't do logo sticker plays," she says. "Instead, we've done really exciting partnerships with people who really want to infuse the blockchain through what they're doing and totally transform their business model."

A good example is Algorand's relationship with the Drone Racing League. DRL is an international community of pilots racing through a course, seeing the race via first-person three-dimensional view of the course at speeds more than 80 mph. It's valued at around $200 million.

DRL has its own Algorand-based, play-to-earn game, built with Playground Labs that is worthy of the metaverse. Players will have actual ownership of the racer's drones and any winnings via NFT's. In September 2021, DRL announced a five-year, $100 million sponsorship from Algorand. "That's a lot different than slapping a name on a jersey," Callaghan notes.

There are other evolutions in gaming being fueled by Algorand. Nick Bucheleres, Taj Tarsha, and

Robert Burden created Smile Coin in 2021 to elimi-nate high fees and slow payment processing in the gaming industry. Their blockchain-based network is "a platform for gamers to manage and control the use of their gaming data and leverage AI-tools to optimize performance." Put simply, Smile is on a mission to decentralize gaming. Their offerings also include streamlined financing for gaming companies and alternatives for payment processing.

Other leading smart contract blockchains couldn't keep up with such a system, so Smile Coin turned to Algorand. Bucheleres says the "cost-effec-tive, scalable, and secure blockchain is the optimal platform to onboard gaming partners within the ecosystem and to act as a bridge to larger non-native blockchain games." They released the SMILE Trans-action Ledger app in 2021.

The pace of Algorand's gaming impact keeps accelerating. In January 2022, the Le Mans Virtual racing esports championship launched an online storefront to host collectable NFTs. These will be video clips and art, encompassing various highlights from the Le Mans Virtual Series and 24-hour virtual races. This will be a first of its kind initiative for this type of an event.

In October 2021, Algorand helped build a bridge between the old-school boardgames and blockchain technology. Sequoia Games uses it as the digital ledger behind its new Flex NBA, a National Basketball Association-licensed boardgame. Players assemble their own roster using physical collectible tiles that represent different NBA players.

Close to my home, Algorand and the female soccer teams NJ/NY Gotham FC announced a multi-year partnership deal in March 2022. As part of the deal, Algorand became the first-ever Official Block-chain and NFT Partner of the National Women's Soccer League club. Gotham FC and Algorand will be unveiling blockchain enabled payments and NFT integrations in-stadium and in the community. "Algorand and Gotham FC share similar mission driven goals, which is what makes this partnership so exciting," said Andrea Pagnanelli, Chief of Business Operations at Gotham FC. "Whether it's blockchain or sports, both of our organizations are committed to empowering women and impacting our community."

The gaming world is evolving quickly, and Algorand is at the forefront. Who says Algos aren't fun?

CHAPTER 4
Those Who Chose Algorand

One of my favorite parts of working at SkyBridge is the opportunity to have conversations with intelligent people. The Algorand community doesn't just attract smart people, it draws principled ones as well. I get invigorated with a feeling of pragmatic optimism whenever I speak to these individuals, and the best way to spread this feeling is to share some of these recent exchanges. These are some with those who chose Algo as the foundation on which to build their futures.

Michael Arrington, Ninor Mansor and Ninos Mansor

Arrington Capital Management

This crypto venture-capital firm in 2022 launched a $100 million fund to back projects building on the Algorand blockchain. The Arrington Algo Growth Fund

(AAGF) contributes to investments to accelerate the development of chains ecosystem, including everything from newly minted NFTs to a partnership with Miami to use Algorand in municipal projects. AAGF is Arrington's second crypto-focused fund after the flagship Arrington XRP Capital Fund; the firm has more than $1 billion in assets under management.

Michael Arrington, former securities lawyer, editor of TechCrunch, and Time Magazine's "One of the World's 100 Most Influential People" in 2008, is a big believer in the power of the blockchain. In 2019 he purchased an Australian company called ByteSize Capital, an innovator in technical due diligence and data science as it applies to crypto markets. ByteSize's founders, twin brothers Ninor and Ninos Mansor (and their proprietary investing suite) joined Arrington Capital as partners.

AS: Why does Algorand have less name recognition than other cryptocurrencies, and is this even a bad thing?

MA: A lot of meme coins are great. They're entertaining and shape culture. Algorand's never done that. I actually think that's part of what has slowed adoption—it's just not as fun. But I don't necessarily think they should just start going crazy with the meme-ing. It just doesn't feel like them, especially not Silvio. Algorand doesn't have the [price] surges and cultural popularity that other coins have, but I actually think in the long run, it's going to work out well for them because this is a serious business.

AS: It can be hard to see how significant and transformative the blockchain can be, with all the noise over the meme coin of the moment.

MA: Last year was the year of people showing they don't care. As long as it works, they're going to get behind a project. The community's gotten so big, so fast and I think many don't know what the world "decentralization" means. Everybody was sort of fine with these networks getting up and running that were very fast, but were in no way, true crypto from a philosophical point of view. Our viewpoint is that, at some point, the other L1s ones are going to trip over themselves. At that point, everyone will start to appreciate the beauty of Algorand, not just in theory, but in reality. That moment hasn't come yet, but we think it's inevitable.

AS: So how did you guys come to discover Algorand?

Ninos: Ninos found the Algorand white paper in early 2018. It seemed at the time that every professor at every university was launching a new chain. But we found it very compelling from a technical perspective. It's very similar to Bitcoin in the sense that Bitcoin could only have been created by Satoshi Nakamoto—that group or person, whoever they are. There was 20 years of cyber punk history, the email list, hashtag cash and all these different iterations of digital money that ended up culminating in BTC. Bitcoin couldn't have existed in any other way. And in the same way, the reaction we had to Algorand is that it could only be created by Silvio Micali. This wasn't a two-year paper; this was the culmination of 30 or 40 years of work.

AS: I'm struck by the way his work with original cryptography research so directly impacts Algorand's approach to the blockchain.

Ninos: All that work in on Byzantine consensus that happened in the seventies, eighties, nineties, it didn't go anywhere in terms of the cryptocurrency space. You're only seeing now the pure applications of say PBT, right. That type of consensus mechanism applied in systems like cosmos. And then it wasn't until Bitcoin came along and it created this sort of permissionless way of achieving consensus. The way I like to characterize it is it's the merger of classical Byzantine agreement and Byzantine consensus with Namo consensus if that makes sense. It's the fusion of these two.

AS: Solana recently suffered an outage. What happened and why is Algorand protected from something similar?

Ninos: Solana's network was basically flooded by a ton of transactions, and they build it with the assumption that there's infinite capacity. And Solana has a lot of apps that produce a lot of transactions. You can essentially submit as many transactions as you want without hitting any fees, so there's no supply and demand balance there. So, when you have these big liquidation events, like you did the other day, when basically every DeFi user is submitting transactions—it overloads the validators themselves.

With Solana, it's kind of like consensus done backwards. What I mean by that is, every node sort of figures out its history of the blockchain by itself. And then every so often they check with each other and say, "Hey, do we have the same thing?" What happens is during these times where it goes down, they all go out of sync, every node doesn't align with the others, and they start dropping transactions.

What you need instead is a system that even if you're pushing up against max capacity, the system itself is resilient to that flood. Algorand has truly decentralized consensus nodes, every round is a different set of validators, so there's no bottleneck.

Niros: Decentralization is like insurance. If Algorand had the same circumstance as Solana, it would at worst just slow down for a bit of time, but you wouldn't fundamentally overwork the network.

AS: And slow for Algorand is still pretty fast, thousands of transactions per second.

Ninos: Exactly. But keep in mind, the reality is no blockchain is good or bad. They just make different tradeoffs. Maybe some chains are countries like Singapore. You know what you're getting, you get sort of this extreme rule of law, but you're living in a dictatorship. And there that sort of system is not scalable; you can't scale it to hundreds of millions of people. On the other hand, maybe you get a system like anarchy, where there's no security, it's completely scalable. You could have anarchy across the entire world, but again, you're trading something off.

The way we put it, Algorand is at a defining moment like the birth of like the American Republic. It was the first socially scalable political system, designed from the ground up for every user to be secure. Every citizen could self-govern and in the same way, just as anyone who owns an Algo can self-govern. But nations are different, too. Some chains could be a great Singapore—they might do something really, really well—high-frequency trading or something. But if you want a system that's a lot more ambitious that can scale to a global level, Algorand is on par with something like American democracy.

AS: Well, Algorand and the American revolution both started in Boston, so maybe the history is rubbing off on you guys.

Ninos: There are all these funny mythologies surrounding that. When you talk to Silvio, he has a lot to say about George Washington; he can sit there and opine on these topics for 10 hours. Whereas the people in other chains are very pragmatic. They're kind of like, 'Okay, there are problems, and we'll solve them one day.' We are building those solutions today. Algorand is a very philosophical chain. Algorand's principled approach is to not make the tradeoffs that other systems make. Maybe that means it takes a little bit longer for things to get off the ground, but long term it makes it stronger.

AS: As an institutionalist, that approach sounds pretty appealing.

Niros: We said, why don't we roll our sleeves up and start a dedicated Arrington Algorand Fund and push the ecosystem support? We've seen how ecosystems grow elsewhere. I think if you can get the same kind of mix of pragmatists and builders, then we'll end up with a foundation that is way more robust in the long term.

AS: How do you see Algorand's adoption unfolding over the next few years?

Niros: The way we think about it, everything that people are chasing in 2021 can and probably will be done on Algorand. The first step is to replicate fast DeFi, literally everything that's been done elsewhere but on a solid and decentralized foundation. And then the other thing we talk about, in parallel, is doing all this work with institutions and bringing on "old world" assets that would only want to be on a decentralized chain because they need that insurance. The ultimate strategy for our brand is when these two worlds meet.

AS: When you're looking at the ways to sort of build out the ecosystem with the Algorand Fund, what do you look for?

MA: That's just the craft of venture investing, which is something I've been doing since I sold Tech Crunch, although I've been in that world my whole career.

AS: Are people lining up, do you actively recruit, and how do you evaluate them?

MA: It's all of the above. Some people reach out to us. Algorand also meets people all the time, and they make introductions to us. The main thing that we can do to be successful as venture capitalists is to treat the companies that we've invested in super well. The best way to get new customers is to treat your existing customers well, and it's also much cheaper to keep a customer than it is to go find a new one.

John Clarke and Owen Colegrove

Algofi

The world of DeFi is stocked with fascinating entrepreneurs. The founders of Algofi are young, whip-smart and convinced that the blockchain will change how the world moves money. Owen Colegrove graduated with a PhD in Particle Physics and did research at the European particle accelerator at the European Organization for Nuclear Research (CERN). John Clarke graduated from MIT with a degree in Math and Computer Science. The pair met at Citadel, where they worked as quantitative strategists until they broke away to pursue crypto. Algofi is building the first crypto native bank powered by decentralized finance. Through Algofi, users can lend cryptocurrency, earn interest on their deposits, and borrow to facilitate complex trading activity. Because Algofi is built on Algorand, they can offer transactions that cost less than $0.01, compared to

$15 or more on other networks. In November 2021 they announced $2.8 million in seed funding led by Union Square Ventures, Arrington XRP Capital, and Pillar VC led the round.

AS: Owen, weren't you a particle physicist? How'd you end up at Algofi?

OC: My background was really in doing data science and extracting insight and knowledge from large data sets. So, that's pretty applicable to finance these days. At Citadel, where I met John, we were making algorithmic trading strategies.

AS: What prompted you guys to start Algofi, and how did you settle on Algorand to build on?

JC: Owen and I left Citadel and we were really interested in DeFi. In 2021 we applied to a startup accelerator, pitching them on this idea that a lot of people own crypto, but it's still hard to access DeFi. We wanted to give more access to this new financial system. This kind of looks like the Internet in 2000, at the very early stages of something that's about to take off and effect positive change on the world.

Our first application was building a way to access Ethereum-based smart contracts. The problem with this experience is that Ethereum is very expensive and slow. So, creating a retail application that can compete with applications like Robinhood, Schwab, or another Fintech, was pretty much impossible. We needed something faster and cheaper.

We looked at a ton of options. Honestly, we spent two weeks doing pretty intense research, looking at the different dimensions of block-chain. Could we see ourselves building there? How innovative do we think the team's going to be? Where is it not just today, but where is it going to be in two or three years? We're kind of hitching ourselves to a wagon when we decide to build somewhere. And I think we looked down along these different axes and the choice at the time was really between Solana and Algorand. And we picked Algorand because we felt like Solana had maybe given up a little bit in terms of reliability and decentralization.

AS: It would appear so, given the slowdowns and pauses.

OC: I think my first instinct is to say when you're in a sea of volatility, try to anchor yourself to something. A lot of people rush after whatever is the hot thing today, but that's fleeting. Our true compass north is where we think value will be. We naturally partner well with Algorand because if we actually believe the level value that is going to come out of this space, their number one mission is working towards that. They're building tech that we think is going to be enduring, and so that makes it a smart bet on a long horizon.

JC: I think it's fair to say that Algorand is focusing more on building good long-term technology instead of flashy things like a lot of marketing. The market assigns a lot of value to marketing instead of tech, but that could change as soon as a couple years from now. As people realize that the other chains can't scale to support activity, we're going to see a drift into chains like Algorand. I think Algorand stands the best chance of winning.

Their big advantage is they're kind of like the adult in the room. They work on relationships with corporations and governments. And this could bear a lot of fruit. If they get a deal with the government to move a lot of value onto the chain, that could be huge.

AS: Will institutional adoption help retail operations like yours?

JC: Locally, we're focusing on the retail. We are going to prove our product works and is safe then the institutions will follow. But if institutions need a different enterprise product to use smart contracts, that's something that we might build out for them. If we think there's a lot of value, if that's another $200 million coming into the protocol, then we would do that.

OC: When Bitcoin came out, the first people were retail, and for a long-time institutions didn't get involved. Well, most institutions are still not involved in crypto. I think we're going to see institutions come into DeFi a lot faster. They saw the returns from others being involved early in crypto, and they don't want to miss out.

JC: I think it comes down to this: If you are convinced that DeFi is growing, and crypto use in general is growing, we're going to see tens of millions of people entering the space. If you are convinced that Ethereum won't be able to scale and other L1s can't really do the job, then Algorand is going to benefit. It might happen faster than we think.

Matt Zhang

Hivemind

Like any community, institutionalists find solace in the company of other institutionalists. Matt Zhang is a visionary institutionalist, the kind of guy I really appreciate. He left China at the age of 18 when he went to universities in London and Cambridge. Zhang spent 15 years on Wall Street, working with Citigroup and moving to New York four years ago. Last October he set out on his own to launch the crypto fund, Hivemind, to make investments in crypto companies, trade digital assets, and pursue dedicated play-to-earn strategies in the gaming space.

AS: What's your aspiration in starting Hivemind?

MZ: If you think about investing, the first names you think of are BlackRock and Blackstone. They are household names; nobody loses their job or sleep investing into a BlackRock fund. We want Hivemind in 5 to 10 years to be the BlackRock for investors wanting exposure to crypto. We want to be among the top three names they think about. When they say, 'We want to allocate 1%, let's go to the pipeline and see who's offering what,' our job is to make sure we're providing the full menu for them to choose from.

AS: Does your background grant you a useful perspective on the crypto market?

MZ: I think I'm unique in that I came from a traditional finance background. I'm 36, I obviously grew up in the mobile internet age. I got a chance to watch, but not really drive the Internet revolution. And I really see crypto and blockchain in general as the next paradigm shift.

AS: How long have you been following Algorand?

MZ: I knew Steve Kokinos for more than three years before the launch. We watched the company grow from scratch and helped them along the way. When it came time to do this full time, you have to ask who you want to team up with. So, in that context, I got to know Algorand very well, and

I wanted them to be very intimately involved in my project.

AS: What appealed to you?

MZ: I asked, how good is their technology? How good is their funding team? How good is their community? Algorand's people are very mature in thinking about the long run, not just the price tomorrow. An institutional quality network with the first-class technology product behind an awesome community which is very loyal and always trying to focus on building stuff is actually very rare.

AS: How integral was Silvio Micali's involvement in Algorand to your adoption of it for Hivemind?

MZ: You just don't get a Turing award winner to be your technology founder every other day, right? If you mention Professor Silvio to people in the space, crypto OGs, they all show great respect. He's a pioneer in zero knowledge proofs. That's what's needed on the technology side...and on your product side. I In my mind, he's a very romantic guy. He thinks about the technology in a pure way.

It may be a cliché to say, but all the money I think is a side product. He already made it, quite frankly, he doesn't need any more. He's still very much focusing on how to perfect a blockchain, like the way Steve Jobs was obsessed with the Apple products.

Then you move to the other folks. Steve Kokinos and Sean Ford. You have the scientist, the startup entrepreneur, and you have Sean's background. I think that really created the right sort of chemistry between the founding team.

AS: What kind of growth is needed for the blockchain to reach its full potential?

MZ: For crypto to become a paradigm shift, it needs to be $50 trillion market. It's close to $1.3 trillion today. So, it's actually still very, very small. The way we're going to get there is for the market to be 50 times bigger, not 50 times higher. There's a big difference here. That money cannot come from retail, it needs to come from people who are still skeptical about getting more familiar with this space, like pensions. But I have a very strong feeling that we are now beyond the inflection point—every single bank is doing their own digital product offering. So, if the money is coming from institutional investors, that's going to make this paradigm shift happen. And for these investors to get involved, they need an institutional quality blockchain to work with. They want to go with somebody that has great credentials and a great product. And I think if you think about it from a market level, Algorand is the best in the space. That's sort of what I see from the Wall Street side.

AS: With a market that vast, there will be room for more than one chain. There will have to be more than one if things develop the way we all hope. So where does Algorand fit in?

MZ: If the market's that big, there are going to be a lot of people doing interesting things. Then I guess the question is, what do *you* want to be focusing on? I genuinely think that, as unsexy as it sounds, you need institutional companies coming in. And I think for you to get Wall Street, pensions, and the like, they'll care about the reliability, speed, security, privacy, they'll care about the issue of quality.

AS: How important is it that Algorand can work with other cryptocurrencies and build bridges in the ecosystem in general, for institutionalists specifically?

MZ: It's super important. If you talk to Silvio, he deeply believes in this, he doesn't want Algorand to be the only one there. If it is, that probably means that the [blockchain] statement itself is false in the first place. To be decentralized, means nobody will control the ecosystem. Everybody participates in a certain way. So, I think if you talk to Silvio and Steve, they don't have the ambition to be the only one.

I want Hivemind to be the crypto Blackstone in five years, remember? I'm betting on the market 50 times bigger. So, I want to create segues to welcome all investors, institutional to retail, to easily find a way to invest in crypto space. And I think institutional investors are a big force to drive this space a lot bigger, which means I want to provide a fuller menu for them to do that. Starting from a stablecoin, offering to trading venture, to ETF, anything offering access to crypto assets in a regulatory compliant way.

AS: A lot of everyday people may not equate high finance with ethics, but it's really at the core of any successful business, especially in an emerging market.

MZ: If you are working in any frontier, artificial intelligence, or spaceflight for example, you have responsibilities to do things the right way because you are one of the few people that can. You are making a kind of mini history in that field. Everything is past dependent; people can follow you or not. I know it's a little cheesy, crypto is not rocket science, but I still feel the goosebumps every day. We actually are able to design a protocol that may change how people pay each other. I mean, that's pretty cool.

David Garcia

Borderless Capital

David Garcia, digital payments specialist and a veteran blockchain entrepreneur formed Borderless Capital in November 2018, before the Algorand MainNet was even live. He's been on board with Algorand since its inception. Since inception, Borderless has invested in more than 100 companies, run four global accelerator programs across Asia, Europe, and North America, and all along the way shepherded the expansion of Algorand. Borderless' ALGO Fund I is supporting the next wave of DeFi on Algorand. Some of the key companies backed by the fund are Tinyman, Yieldly.Finance, Reach, AlgoMint, Runtime Verification, HummingBot, HexTrust, Opulous, Xfinite, Six Clovers, Securitize, BlockDaemon, IntoTheBlock, Flare Network, Osprey Funds, Floating Point Group, and Artory.

AS: You saw the opportunity in crypto well before most.

DG: I have a strong background in online payments and digital payments, especially in emerging markets. I have seen all the frictions, all the complexity, all the problems that the traditional payments systems have. I have been working as an entrepreneur in blockchain since 2013. In 2015, I started to operate as an investor in the blockchain space. Bitcoin was $300 and Ethereum was $18 at the time. Everyone thought that I was crazy, but since then, it seems they were wrong.

Back in the day, when I saw the power of the blockchain—that you can send money from my home country, Argentina, to Shanghai in three minutes for a fraction of a cent—I thought, 'This is a solution for a lot of the problems that we have right now in the current payment system.' But as there was more adoption of the technology, I became aware of its problems. I have seen all of these different imperfect approaches to a technology that should be solving a big problem of society.

AS: Did you recognize Algorand was different in its early days?

DG: When I first heard about Silvio, I was investing in different Layer-1's. One of my investors was close to the MIT club and set up a meeting. I took a call with Silvio in November 2017. He explained how novel the consensus was that he wanted to build. I had that "Aha!" moment that I had five years before, when I started in blockchain. So, in June 2018 I decided to do a large investment in Algorand. I wrote one of the largest checks that I have ever invested in a Layer-1 blockchain. As I kept learning about Algorand, I decided that I didn't want to distract myself with anything else.

AS: What are your observations on Algorand's growth and development?

DG: There was a plan that was promised in the white paper that Silvio wrote, and we have not been disappointed. Since the network was live, there has not been any downtime. There have not been slow downs in block productions, more and more features are coming to the stack. And that is allowing a lot of entrepreneurs, a lot of fans of the technology, a lot of developers to come and build amazing things. The network is getting more popular and busier every day.

AS: What are you looking for from companies you invest in?

DG: It's a combination of things. There are a lot of amazing ideas and disruptive business models that people were trying to build on the blockchain but the core technology of those blockchains was not allowing these applications to go to the mainstream. They could never create a critical mass of users. So, what we're looking for now is the same business models and for the same product but to be able to scale mainstream adoption.

Algorand is also a great technology for trading and moving value across the world, for anything related to payments or financial services. We are seeing a lot of projects that were not possible in other blockchains because they don't have the right primitives.[4] Algorand has the right technology primitives that will enable friction-less transactions, like their atomic transfers. With one transaction, you can exchange multiple assets.

AS: What does Algorand need to focus on to improve?

DG: I think that we should spend much more resources and time bringing developers into the community. In reality, who will move the needle to critical mass will be the developers. We need hundreds of thousands of developers right now building on Algorand, something that we are struggling with a little bit more than other blockchains, but we are getting there.

AS: It seems as though Algorand has an ideal, built-in messenger for this in Silvio Micali.

---

4   Primitives are the algorithms that are frequently used to build cryptographic protocols for computer security systems. Micali is a maestro of cryptographic primitives.

DG: I was there for his keynote speech at Decipher in Miami. It created goosebumps for everyone that was there. It was the first time that we saw the founder speaking about the technology that he created, speaking to the community with his heart in his hands. I think he should continue to do that. Silvio is the father of the modern cryptography, the father of the privacy, the father of using technology for respecting human rights. He asks, why spend so many billions of dollars on transaction fees when we can have a technology that can bring all that value back to the humankind? He's the right person to attract all the blockchain developers, all the crypto geeks that are in other blockchains. I think that he shares the same passion that those people have.

Micali in Miami

On November 29, 2021, Silvio Micali appeared at the company's Decipher conference in Miami. In a speech introduced by Mayor Francis Suarez, he put forth his vision.

Good morning, everyone. Thank you, Mayor Suarez, and thank you Miami for your vision and your warm hospitality. And thank you Algonauts everywhere.

We should be proud of all we have accomplished. After two and a half years from our launch, with over 17 million blocks produced and with over 1000 companies building on Algorand, let's take a moment to reflect why we are here and what we want to be.

Algorand is here to bring true decentralization. All blockchains talk about decentralization, all blockchains talk about financial inclusion. Talk is cheap, we deliver.

In a centralized, or poorly centralized blockchain, an elite club has always had the power to exclude anyone they want from the economy. We are here to put an end to this. Algorand exists to make it easy and cheap to participate. This is true decentralization, and true decentralization is essential to financial inclusion.

Financial inclusion also requires scalability, because there are billions of us, and because each one of us wants to, and should be able to transact. Blockchains that support 16 transactions per second cannot guarantee any financial inclusion; at the most, they can support speculation.

Algorand is here because we finally guarantee decentralization and scalability. We have worked very hard to build our beautiful home and we are here to protect it.

Before Algorand, people believed it was impossible for a blockchain to be simultaneously decentralized, scalable, and secure. We are here because we can tell the difference between impossible and hard, and because we can take apart what is hard.

Algorand is here because our technology works. Since our launch, we have produced block after block every 4.4 seconds, without interruptions and without any forks. Other blockchains halt routinely, thinking nothing of half-day downtime every month.

Such a level of service may be fine for speculation. Blockchain is down? I'll speculate tomorrow. But for basic services, financial services, healthcare services, air quality monitoring, and so on, it's a different story. We are here because continuity of service is crucial.

Algorand is here because we can upgrade, have upgraded, and will continue to upgrade our platform.

Whenever blockchains tell you, "We are proud that the chain will continue to operate in the same way it has always operated", walk away.

When they announce year after year an improvement that never comes, stop paying attention.

Access to better technology is our rightful expectation. When new and safe technology becomes available and we agree to incorporate it, Algorand will incorporate it seamlessly and without any interruption of service as we have done so far, and as we will continue to do.

Nothing static lives for very long or remains relevant for a very long. Life is about intelligent adaptation. We are here to adopt intelligently and together; we shall leave no one technologically behind.

The traditional economy is built on expensive mediators who do not care nor have financial incentive to secure ordinary transactions of ordinary people; a mediator that adds value to a transaction is always welcome. But when the only function of a mediator is to make the transaction itself possible, then what is welcome is a secure technology that replaces that mediator.

Consider a bilateral exchange: you have an asset that I want, I have an asset that you want, and we want to swap them. This is the cornerstone of trade; it must be secure, convenient, and cheap. Even if it costs 50 cents, it costs too much, because 50 cents is an exorbitant amount when your salary is $100 a month or when the assets to be exchanged are worth 10 bucks.

In Algorand, a bilateral exchange is implemented as a single indivisible transaction in less than five seconds at the cost of a fraction of a cent and writing a single line of code.

Financial inclusion requires such super efficiency. Algorand is here because we can finally provide it.

Algorand is here because it is the ideal platform for decentralized autonomous organization. We have seen enough wrongs in our lives, and we should right as many as we can.

You want to launch a DAO [decentralized autonomous organization] because you want to enable your community to organize itself in new and better ways, preventing centralization in other inequities from popping up again.

But launching a decentralized organization in a centralized blockchain makes no sense. You want to launch your DAO on Algorand, because Algorand stands for and operates by your same principles.

A few days ago, 51,000 Algorand governors voted in a crucial governance vote. No DAO in any blockchain has ever seen such a level of participation. Algorand is here to sustain this in much higher levels of participation.

Algorand is here because we are the green blockchain. Some blockchains consume as much electricity as a small country. Algorand only uses the energy needed to power 10 homes. Being green is our pride and our moral obligation. The less privileged are first to suffer from the degradation of the environment. A blockchain that is bad for the environment is a bad blockchain, period.

Algorand is green by design. We have been green from day one and we shall continue to be green. That's why projects like Planet Watch and Climate Trade have chosen to build on and are thriving on Algorand.

Technology is quintessentially human. When we built our first tool, we became more, not less human. But our human journey has been a torturous one. Time and again, we have lost our way in some very dark places. And technology was also used to oppress people to deprive us of our humanity.

Even today, technology that enables us to stay in touch with our friends also demands that we surrender our information about ourselves. Really? I think it's time to turn this business plan on its head.

Yes, there is technology for bad, which is why we must create better technology for good. Let's leverage our great technology to express our consent. If we want to consent, to specify the type of advertising information we are willing to receive and the price we demand for the privilege to bring such information to our attention. Let's leverage our technology to retain control of our information.

Algorand will reframe the concept of ownership of our personal information in what we create; that is why Algorand is here.

Let me share with you something personal. I was born in Palermo, Sicily, but I spent my childhood in Agrigento. Two thousand five hundred years ago, Agrigento was a famous Greek city, Agragas. At the time, Agragas was known to be the most beautiful city of the mortals. It's temple of Zeus, now destroyed, was bigger than the Parthenon in Athens.

But when I arrived on the scene, Agrigento was the poorest province of Italy. Yet it retained visible memory of its glorious past: its temples. Agregento temples lie in majestic procession on a hillcrest against the backdrop of the blue Mediterranean Sea. They were—and still are—magnificent.

Let me date myself. When I was a kid over 60 years ago, travel was hard; no credit cards, no travel checks, cash only. Minimal hotel reception at Agregento, scant transportation too, yet nothing could stop people from rushing to the temples by taxi, by car, on horseback, on foot, from everywhere in all stations in life.

Everybody, local farmers, romantic foreigners, local fishermen, archeologists, you name it, everybody got their beauty.

All new couples from all socioeconomic strata wanted to memorialize their wedding day next to the creation of artists dead for over two millennia, yet still capable of inspiring us. That's when I understood the true power of art. We are the art we make and will be remembered by the art we leave behind for everyone to enjoy like the light of the sun.

So why is it the current economic structure stacked against the artist?

Never mind, let's look forward and let's change history. We humans are creators, we create technology, and we create art. Personally, I am a technologist, but very much an admirer of the transforming power of art.

In Algorand, we finally have a platform that allows us to make it right for artists, to enable more artists to have sustainable careers, to focus on their art rather than on a multiplicity of side jobs, and to make the self-releasing of art effective and efficient.

Algorand and art should be more than an end, it should be a perfect union.

(Crowd applause.)

There it is, plain and simple. Algorand will be the backbone of the new creator economy. In this new economy, new social behavior will emerge. All artists dialogue with prior artists, all poets respond to prior poets, and musicians routinely re-interpret prior tunes. With Algorand, artists finally have the right technology to share credit and money with those who've inspired their work.

Even if one download of your song generates 25 cents in Algorand, you have the option—at the cost of a fraction of 1 cent—to automatically give some of your hard earned 25 cents to those who have inspired your work and helped you reach your perfect audience.

Not because of some contracts—sometimes the source of our inspiration is so deep in our souls that only we can recognize it—but because people who love you and your work will love you more for it, because it is the right thing to do, and because with Algorand we can finally afford doing the right thing.

With Algorand, the artistic community has the ability to re-organize itself in new and better ways, in a fair DAO, where the artists sit at the table, in fact, at the head of a table, a cooperative table, a self-governing table, in which everyone has a say.

Art is more than a collection of separate individuals; it is a social endeavor. Algorand is here to provide the tool to make this social endeavor fair and to create a world in which the artists want to create.

So where are we? We are here. This is a statue by Michelangelo. It has been cataloged as "unfinished work." To me, it perfectly captures us at this point of our journey.

After a titanic struggle, we are slowly but surely extricating ourselves from all this mass of garbage that has piled upon and imprisoned us for too long. It is about time we break free and break free we shall, for we have things to say, energies to express, and beautiful things to create.

So, let's enjoy this beautiful meeting, let's bond with one another, let's gather our strength, and then let's make a difference for our planet, for all who have been excluded from finance and for all who are voiceless in the matters of their own creation.

We have the tools, we have the vision, and we have the determination; we shall prevail. Go Algorand!

CHAPTER 5
Planet Algorand

So far, we have spoken mainly about Algorand Inc., the tech company that operates out of the United States. It manages the Layer-1 protocol, building out iterations of it, like any other product pipeline. However, there is also a non-profit, the Algorand Foundation.

The Algorand Foundation is based in Singapore and with an international board of directors it is responsible for nurturing the ecosystem. The Foundation runs hackathons to garner coders' interest and offers grants to entrepreneurs building apps. The Foundation offers a $250,000 bounty for indie developers who want to integrate blockchain functionality into their existing games—or build a new one that uses NFTs (like card games) or is set in the metaverse. The hackathon is called "Bring Your A Game."

The Algorand Centers of Excellence program is a call for development proposals from university students around the world. The Foundation also tries to build bridges to other blockchains.

Staci Warden, the Foundation's CEO, sees a world she dubs "Planet Algorand," as "a metaverse where people bike everywhere, it's totally carbon neutral and people are nice to each other, everything about a community that we want to be."

Warden is equal parts dreamer and financial strategist. She spent much of career focused on capital market development and financial inclusion within developing countries. She worked as an executive director at J.P. Morgan for eight years before joining the non-profit Milken Institute from 2013 to 2021. At the Milken Institute, she started researching crypto and fell in love with the concept, mostly because she could so easily see the benefits that the blockchain brings to developing countries. In fact, Warden once said, "It's just crazy that you can send a movie from Nigeria to Malaysia, but you can't send five bucks instantaneously.... I saw that this [crypto] might be a solution."

Over the years, Warden's status in the crypto world grew, promoting the blockchain within the Milken Institute and attending the exclusive annual MOBILE Blockchain Summit at Richard Branson's Necker Island. She was increasingly taken by the ways the blockchain could be leveraged to solve real problems; her passion was exhibited when she discussed how "people talk about the dark web, ransomware and all of that stuff, but the other side of that same coin is an Afghan woman being able to keep her savings away from her husband and father.... It's someone being able to control their own financial future."

In 2021, headhunters called Warden to recruit her to the Foundation's board of directors. She recalls "asking people about what they thought about Algorand...And a lot of people that knew a lot about crypto had kind of no idea what I was talking about."

Warden herself had to dive deeply into the Algorand blockchain to become more familiar with it, and she was excited by Micali's solution. "The idea that he had come up with something that, if you look at it, it's so obvious. That this protocol was not on the top 10, I just couldn't believe it," she said "I thought to myself, 'This is the best tech. It can't be hard to do something about making this ecosystem more well-known.'"

Warden saw that the impact Algorand has on lives is real. The Algorand Foundation has partnerships with organizations such as Women's World Banking, Save the Children in the Philippines, and several other relief organizations in the United States. The Foundation is engaged in a pilot program with a mobile phone operator in Africa creating blockchain payment plans for mobile phones.

Algorand, the tech company, has several cryptographers and scientists. Separately, the Foundation has its own division of impressive cryptographers, including Hugo Krawczyk and Craig Gentry. Michael Arrington has said, "There are a bunch of all-star cryptographers and engineers at the Algorand Foundation that nobody knows about.... They are these hidden hero superstars. They deserve so much credit."

Warden accepted a board position, and within a year she had been tapped to become the Foundation's CEO. As a result, you can anticipate Algorand to have a higher profile and more developer interest, wallets, and dApps on its network. Warden says, "It's not about the price of the Algo. It's about building up Planet Algorand so that people are participating.... We are going to put in motion a longer-term strategy around impact and inclusion, because that's very important to us. We are going to double our head count maybe almost [to about 25] and we're talking about quadrupling our community engagement managers."

A welcome change will be the emphasis on marketing at the Foundation. Warden claims that "One of the sins that that the Algorand Foundation made in the beginning is that, because they had the best tech by an order of magnitude, everybody just thought that the truth would speak for itself.... I think that was in error. The Foundation must be visible in the ecosystem. It's about getting the word out, engaging with the community and making sure we tell the story."

Warden's biggest dreams for social justice will need a robust token to manifest. She claims that "the idea of inclusion at scale, globally, is only going to happen on the Algorand blockchain. None other has the capacity to do it. This is our game to win and it's our field to win on."

Built to Last

We live in a disposable society. Things made today do not seem to be made to last. Shoe repair shops are fading before shelves of mass-produced footwear; milk bottles became cartons destined for landfills; mobile phones are tossed when the new model arrives, or when their screens crack.

In an increasingly digital world, which is changing quickly and furiously, this trend of disposable thinking seems likely to keep increasing. Things already travel quicker than the speed of social media, often rewarding those who bring heat but little light. What will have value in a metaverse, where nothing is tangible, and everything is immediate? What is good in designing anything for the digital world that persists, when the whole point is to always be new?

I argue that it is more important than ever to build our digital world with a sense of permanency and stability. Real change does not just come from the chaos of creation, it comes from the more somber concepts of planning, patience, and discipline.

I spoke to Silvio Micali about this theory recently, and true to romantic form, it made him think of his home in Italy. As a boy, he would admire the temples and aqueducts that still stood after thousands of years. He points out that these were not built by luck, and he can recite intimate details about the Romans' use of iron fittings to hold the structures in place. These efforts preserved the structures during the ensuing centuries of earthquakes and weathering. These structures were designed to endure, with the skills needed to ensure they would survive for future generations.

Blockchains should not just connect Point A to Point B today, like a poorly built aqueduct. They should be solid foundations upon which the future can flourish. That does not happen by accident in crypto any more than it happens in architecture. Someone must choose to put forth the vision of something more stable and scalable and stick to it.

As much as a visionary is needed—a chief architect, if you will—the communal spirit that created the Catholic cathedrals of Italy becomes a metaphor for Micali as well. Micali says that "If you look [at] those big cathedrals, they were paid [for] by the citizens of a tiny Republic who decided to tax themselves for something that was going to be built over four or five generations. It takes social pride to do something like that together.... I'm very proud to build such a cathedral—and that's what Algorand is, in the scope of work, in the personal sacrifice, in its ability to inspire other people to build on it, and to put their hopes, dreams and treasure into something that will help all humanity."

The idea that crypto could bring a permanent benefit to billions of people is not Algorand's alone. Much of the crypto world shares this philosophy and has engineered various tokens to get there. Micali is not cutthroat about competing coins—he appreciates the energy of the community. "What I like about this blockchain movement is that there are people who really believe in decentralization and in the end want to get this power to us collectively," Micali says. "I don't see them as competitors. I see them as likeminded people who want to do it in their own way. And that's why our next project at Algorand is really to build decentralized bridges between blockchains."

It is a fascinating idea, and one built on humility. If tokens are automobiles, some are built for speed and some for security. The fastest cars can be used for racing, the slower buses for school children. They are built for a purpose, and trade off abilities based on their use cases. A fast blockchain could be great for high frequency trading, but not as well suited for institutional use (like banking) that usually prizes security over speed. "Some blockchains are going to be better at some things than another," Micali says. "So, what we want to do is to have a network that connects all of us, so that you can transfer assets and take advantage of a better technology wherever it is."

Planning for a future that accommodates your competitors is mature, collegial, and smart. The crypto community has a lot to lose by eating itself and everything to gain by collaborating. A future with just one cryptocurrency is not one where the blockchain revolution is going well. The opportunities are too vast for there to be only one.

This leads to an interesting point in life for Silvio Micali, who at the time of publication is 67 years old. For much of his career, he worked alone, only taking one student at a time "because [he is] so obsessed about solving one problem at a time and by definition, you cannot be obsessed about two problems," he says. Micali explains that "This started as a solitary venture, just me locked in a room. I learned how much better we can join to make something, instead of any single individual."

Now, Micali is at the forefront of the blockchain movement, leading a team that is poised to change the industry at a fundamental level. His days are filled with conversations, decisions, debates, introductions, and projections. He aims to appear at more conferences, facing competitors and allies alike.

"I'm having the time of my life," Micali says. "This for me has been a big adventure, as all things are."

New Crypto World

By now, you have heard the arguments and met the people who convinced me that Algorand is here to stay. Some have a developer's eye view, some are focused on retail, and others are squarely fixed on getting the attention of big institutions. When it comes to Algorand adoption, everyone has their own version of who will blow up the token first. Here is how I think the future is going to work.

A combination of retail and younger people is going to make it happen. The 28-year-olds are already comfortable with Bitcoin and digitization. They are already living in the metaverse. By the time they're 38, they are totally immersed. It is a combination of demographic comfort, with old timers with old technologies leaving the system.

The advantages of the blockchain will not happen exclusively on a financial level. Instead, there will be everyday people paying for things, large international deals that create jobs and wealth, families in foreign lands being better supported by their overseas kin, new ways to reach out to artists you appreciate, and easier ways to launch independent businesses. It will be felt everyday by everyone. It is an inherently hopeful business model, and that is what attracts the best people to it.

What is starting to happen is this communal discovery of this great protocol known as Algorand. Schumacher's building on it, Arrington's building on it and Garcia's building on it. So where does it fit into the crypto community of the future?

I see Bitcoin as the apex predator, cementing its status as a true store of value. If it really scales beyond our wildest dreams, it becomes the global currency, just as the dollar right now is the global fiat currency. Today, we have the Japanese Yen and the British pound. Tomorrow's equivalents, Algorand, Ethereum, and Solana will be like different currencies, used for specific cases.

This adoption has happened with cloud computing services. You have the Amazon cloud, with certain companies gravitating towards it for its technical properties. You have the Microsoft Cloud and the cloud at IBM. Everyone has a little bit different of a service module. Algorand has, in my opinion, the broadest application. There will be a heavy volume of financial services transactions on it. The great thing is that you could eventually run all financial services off Algorand because it is incredibly secure. As Silvio once said to me, "I want you to imagine every second that [has] elapsed since the creation of the universe, 14 plus billion years ago, every second that's elapsed to 1 is the mathematical possibility of cracking Algorand. That's how secure it is."

Other Layer-1's, like Solana and Ethereum, are doing very exciting things with their communities, but to really get the corporate community, you are going to need something like Algorand. No one does it better than they do. The largest companies in the world are going to want to work on the most secure platform.

Inventors can create a technology, but the people who benefit from it also must discover it. The horse and carriage transitioned into the horseless carriage, but there were still horses out there for a long time. It does not all happen at once and it takes fortitude to stay focused on what can be collectively gained.

The Algorand community has dubbed themselves "Algonauts." I think this title is very fitting, as it compares this community to a band of Greek heroes; Algorand is not just a token, it is also an epic quest.

If every discovery is a journey that individuals must make, then I hope this book has been a map that leads you to a ship called Algorand. Many other Algonauts have already climbed on board and will be thrilled to see you.

GLOSSARY

Address: A string of letters and numbers which a token can be sent to and from.

Algo: The native token (coin) of the Algorand blockchain. As such, the Algo has all the key features of the chain itself.

Blockchain: The blockchain is a public record of transactions in chronological order. The blockchain is shared between users and used to verify the permanence of transactions.

Block: A record in the blockchain that contains and confirms many waiting transactions.

Cryptocurrency: Digital currency that is based on mathematics and uses encryption techniques to regulate the creation of units of currency as well as verifying the transfer of funds. Cryptocurrencies operate independently of a central bank.

Cold Storage: The storage of cryptocurrency private keys in any fashion that is disconnected from the internet. Typical cold storage includes USB drives, offline computers, or paper wallets.

Decentralized: To be without a central authority or controlling party. Bitcoin is a decentralized network since no company, government, or individual is in control of it.

Decentralized Applications (dApps): Software applications built out of smart contracts, often integrated with user-facing interfaces using traditional web technology.

Decentralized Autonomous Organizations (DAOs): Entities whose rules are defined and enforced in the form of smart contracts.

Digital Assets: Tokens representing value that can be traded or transferred within a blockchain network. Bitcoin and other cryptocurrencies were the first blockchain-based digital assets. Others have a range of intended functions beyond payments.

Distributed: A distributed network is designed so that there is no central server or entity that others must connect to. Instead, network participants connect directly to each other.

Governance Systems: Software-based mechanisms that manage changes to smart contracts or other blockchain protocols, often based on tokens that allocate voting rights to stakeholders.

HODL: Hold On for Dear Life. HODL became synonymous for an approach to cryptocurrency investing that shuns trading based on short-term price moves.

Layers: There are two primary ways to achieve blockchain scalability: Layer-1 and Layer-2 solutions. Layer-1 adds utility to a native blockchain to optimize its performance. Layer-2 solutions are third-party protocols that integrate with an underlying Layer-1 blockchain to increase transactional throughput.

Open Source: Software whose code is made publicly available and that is free to distribute. Bitcoin is an open-source project and arguably the first open-source money.

Payment Rail: A platform or a network that moves money from a payer to a payee. Either party, consumer, or business, are able to move funds. Blockchain is a new payment rail, and so are centralized electronic payment systems like PayPal, Venmo, and Zelle.

Peer to Peer: A type of network where participants communicate directly with each other rather than through a centralized server.

Private Key: A string of letters and numbers that can be used to spend Bitcoins associated with a specific Bitcoin address.

Signature: A cryptographic signature is a mathematical mechanism that allows someone to prove ownership.

Smart Contracts: Blockchain-based software code that carries out, controls, and documents relevant events and actions according to predefined terms and rules.

Stablecoins: Digital assets whose values are pegged to a fiat currency, a basket of fiat currencies or other stable-value assets.

Oracles: Data feeds that allow information from sources off the blockchain, such as the current price of a stock or a fiat currency, to be integrated into DeFi services.

Wallets: Software for users to manage assets stored on a blockchain. With a non-custodial wallet, the user has exclusive control of funds through their private keys. With custodial wallets, private keys are managed by a service provider.

ACKNOWLEDGMENTS

I would like to personally thank the entire Algorand team, especially Silvio Micali, Steve Kokinos, and Sean Ford. The Algorand team has done a brilliant job of laying out one of the most amazing technologies of our time. Additionally, I would like to thank Joe Pappalardo for his help in putting the draft together and Ian Kleinert, who, as always, helps me to get the book published. Lastly, I would like to thank Debra Englander who has had the unfortunate circumstance of working with me on almost every one of my books since 2010. I drive Debra crazy but I hope she thinks it's worth it. I would also like to give a shout out to Brett Messing, John Svolos, John Darsie, Samantha Darsie, Deidre Scaramucci, and the entire team at SkyBridge for helping me build a very exciting cryptocurrency business. It has been a difficult time in the markets but I have no doubt that it will be a very rewarding decision to go into Algorand and other crypto currencies. Our best days lie ahead of us. These technologies like Algorand will create incredible economic efficiencies for a next generation of people living in the global economy.

ABOUT THE AUTHOR

Author photo by Deborah Copaken

Anthony Scaramucci is the founder and Managing Partner of Skybridge Capital, a global alternative investment advisory firm. As of June 2021, the firm has $6.4B under management. More than a decade ago he founded and launched the annual SALT conference, a gathering of business leaders, politicians, athletes, and entertainers. He started his career at Goldman Sachs in 1989 and was appointed Vice President of Wealth Management there in 1993. Scaramucci attended Tufts University and Harvard Law School. He served as White House communications director briefly in 2017.

CPSIA information can be obtained
at www.ICGtesting.com
Printed in the USA
JSHW031718030922
29957JS00003B/10